SZN

of

CH▲NGE

Books may be purchased in quantity and/or special sales by contacting the publisher.

Mynd Matters Publishing
715 Peachtree Street NE
Suites 100 & 200
Atlanta, GA 30308
www.myndmatterspublishing.com

978-1-948145-77-0 (pbk)
978-1-948145-78-7 (hdcv)
Library of Congress Control Number: 2020904487

FIRST EDITION

Printed in the United States of America

SZN *of* CH▲NGE

the competitor's playbook
for joy on the path to victory

HANNAH GORDON

MYND
MATTERS

Dear Reader,

Welcome! I can't wait to start this eight-week season with you. I hope you come out of it with the vision, plan, and mental toughness to be a champion in whatever you do, personally or professionally.

This guided journal is a condensed version of the practices that helped me transition from an abuse survivor to a woman who reached the executive ranks of a male-dominated industry by age thirty-five. As someone who worked everywhere from a locker room to a board room, I was often asked how to survive and thrive in any environment—including those that were not designed to accommodate my existence. When I answered, I found myself giving people exercises to do. I realized I wanted to share more than would fit on one page and in one conversation.

SZN of Change was born of my desire to not only answer the question of how to succeed, but also to provide a tangible way to help others find and implement the answer in their own lives and in their own way. More than a survival guide, this is a training tool for living your best life and becoming your best self in the process of achieving your dreams.

The content in *SZN of Change* is the result of a lifetime of learning from trial and error and experience, reading books and articles, being around the best human-performance experts in professional sports, girlfriends, coaches, mentors, and from yoga, dance, science, and prayer. I figured out what worked for me and what was not a fit. The journey to this point was not always pretty. There were days when I wanted to quit, moments when I doubted the vision, times I had to remove people from my life and face fears that made me physically ill.

The exercises are the daily practices I have developed over time with quotes that inspired me, and I hope they will light a spark in you, as well. While I find writing is best as a daily practice, figure out what works best for you. The exercises build on one another, because it takes time to develop a habit of journaling. Commit to the process. Find a pace that works for you and decide up front not to get overwhelmed and quit.

This journal is structured into eight weeks.

Week 1 - Film Study

To get where you want to go, you must first know yourself and where you are today. It is important to review the film (just like athletes, coaches, and scouts) because self-knowledge is the foundation of all success.

Week 2 - Vision

Visualize where you want to go.

Week 3 - Game Plan

Set an actionable game plan for achieving your vision.

Week 4 - Evaluate Your Team

Evaluate the team around you to determine who plays what role and whom you should cut from or add to your roster.

Week 5 - Reading the Clips

Learn how to categorize and process four types of information: useful, constructive criticism; the "warm fuzzies" of positive feedback that lift us when we are down; the "bulletin board material" when our opponents motivate us through their hate; and the "noise" we need to tune out.

Week 6 - In-Game Adjustments

Respond to new information, challenges, and changing circumstances by staying agile and adjusting the game plan.

Week 7 - Recovery

Build your mental toughness through recovery practices of self-care.

Week 8 - Practice

Reinforce regular habits of gratitude, focus, and affirmation to carry on after this season.

At the end of each week, you will encapsulate what you have discovered.

Whether you use *SZN of Change* solo or in a group, I hope you finish this season inspired and the momentum it creates continues as a force in your life. Every exercise is meant to serve and support you, and I look forward to celebrating your successes. Let me know how things are going along the way by using #sznofchange.

With love,

Hannah

Week 1

FILM STUDY

> "We are not God. We are simply the image of God and our task is gradually to discover that image and set it free."
> -Michel Quoist

Film don't lie. Players, coaches, and scouts watch film to study and assess. You're going to start by watching your "film"—studying yourself and making an honest assessment. Everything in your path flows from you. I have seen the most talented people in the world never achieve their potential because they could not take an honest look in the mirror. I risked the same until I did the ugly, hard work. If you want to be a leader, committing to self-exploration is even more imperative. You cannot be a good leader if you have not taken the time to get to know your own strengths and weaknesses, to know your values, and be comfortable in your own skin. This week's exercises focus on self-reflection as we learn to be aware of our feelings, beliefs, values, and strengths. This week you will also start two daily practices: gratitude and free writing.

Gratitude prevents you from quitting because it helps you see your blessings rather than being caught up in the negative. It breaks up your thinking. If you need help finding things for which to be grateful, look around you. Are you breathing? Well, that's something to celebrate.

The "Thoughts, feelings, ideas, reflections" sections provide space for you to use as you wish. Keep a list of ideas, write down your schedule for the day, or use it for general journaling. Whatever you do, I challenge you to fill the entire space. If you feel stuck, keep the pen moving until you cover the page with whatever pops into your head. It doesn't have to be perfect. Free writing keeps your creative juices flowing. We all need creativity to make big plans and solve problems.

Today, I am grateful for:

Thoughts, feelings, ideas, reflections.

"Gratitude is happiness doubled by wonder."
-Gilbert Chesteron

I am grateful for:

I feel:

I feel this in my Body as (e.g., my face is hot, my stomach is in a knot):

Thoughts, feelings, ideas, reflections:

"People can never get better without knowing what they know and feeling what they feel."
-Elvin Semrad

I am grateful for:

I know:

Thoughts, feelings, ideas, reflections:

"At the center of your being, you have the answer;
you know who you are and you know what you want."

-Lao Tzu

I am grateful for:

My values (if you get stuck there are many lists online):

Thoughts, feelings, ideas, reflections:

"I rent my title. I own my character.
My [employer] owns the title. I choose to show up with my ownable
assets, which is my passion, my character."
- Thasunda Brown Duckett

I am grateful for:

Take 10 deep breaths. Listen for the small, still voice within. Did it have anything to share today?

Thoughts, feelings, ideas, reflections:

"The more faithfully you listen to the voice within you,
the better you will hear what is happening outside."

-Dag Hammarskjold

I am grateful for:

Beliefs I am letting go of:

Beliefs I am embracing; I believe:

Thoughts, feelings, ideas, reflections:

"You do not get what you hope for. You do not get what you wish for.
You get what you believe."

-Oprah

I am grateful for:

My fearless expression of my potential.

Thoughts, feelings, ideas, reflections.

"To know yourself is to be confident.
To be confident is to fearlessly express your potential."
-Andy Puddicombe

SELF-SCOUTING REPORT

my values, my strengths, things I love about myself
(write, draw, or collage)

Week 2

VISION

Congratulations on making it through the first (and hardest) week! When my life is out of alignment, I want to stop journaling because I am avoiding truths I don't want to deal with (especially if a relationship is not serving me). If you feel that way, keep writing.

Once you know who you are, you can set the vision of where you want to go.

This week focuses on vision and layers in a new daily practice: affirmation. You will see this as the prompt "I am." Affirmations get your mind right. If you are having trouble with an affirmation, write down what you fear or feel insecure about and then write down the affirmation that offers an opposing perspective. For example, if you feel anxious, your affirmation might be "I am confident" or "I am courageous" or "I am calm as a cucumber and cool as the other side of the pillow." There are no limits on affirmations. Write as many different ones as you like or write the same one over and over again. If it feels silly or untrue, keep going. You are training your mind for a champion's mindset.

I am grateful for:

I am:

Thoughts, feelings, ideas, reflections:

"If we understood the power of our thoughts, we would guard them more closely. If we understood the awesome power of our words, we would prefer silence to almost anything negative. In our thoughts and words, we create our own weaknesses and our own strengths. Our limitations and joys begin in our hearts. We can always replace negative with positive."

-Betty Eadie

I am grateful for:

I am:

If money were no object, I would:

Thoughts, feelings, ideas, reflections:

"Throw your dreams into space like a kite, and you do not know what it will bring back, a new life, a new friend, a new love, a new country."

-Anais Nin

I am grateful for:

I am:

If I were not too old, I would:

Thoughts, feelings, ideas, reflections:

"But do you know the age I will be if I ...?
Yes, the same age you will be if you don't."
- Julia Cameron

I am grateful for:

I am:

If I weren't afraid I'm too

_____

*to*_____,

I would:

Thoughts, feelings, ideas, reflections:

"It is never too late to be what you might have been."
-George Eliot

I am grateful for:

I am:

My dream is:

Thoughts, feelings, ideas, reflections:

"I'm not living the dream because I'm special. I'm living the dream because I was obedient to the call of the dream."

-Oprah

I am grateful for:

I am:

I'm not ready to say it out loud, But:

Thoughts, feelings, ideas, reflections:

"Ideas are most vulnerable in their infancy. When you tell people, you spend all your energy explaining and defending your idea."

-Sara Blakely

I am grateful for:

I am:

What does accomplishing my dream(s) feel like, look like, smell like, and taste like?

Thoughts, feelings, ideas, reflections:

"I only imagined myself winning so it wasn't a surprise."

-Patricio Manuel

MY VISION
(summarize, draw, collage)

Week 3

GAME PLAN

Now that you have a vision and have spoken life into that vision, it's time for a game plan to execute the vision. This week, you will create your game plan.

As you design the game plan, you will layer in the final daily practice: focus. When you see the word "focus" on the page, set an intention or priority for the day. Focusing on one thing to accomplish or an intention for the day sets the tone and helps you achieve your long-term goals. Setting a focus for your day allows you to prioritize and make decisions more efficiently. Your focus may be general or specific. For example, if the vision that most requires your attention in life right now is living healthy, your focus might be "my health" or as wide as "loving myself" or as specific as "drink three liters of water today." As you go about your day, you can then make choices based on your focus of self-love, health, or work towards the specific accomplishment regarding hydration.

Experiment with what works best for you. You can apply these principles whether the area of focus is in the areas of work, school, spirit, or relationships, as well.

I am grateful for:

I am:

Focus for the day:

Thoughts, feelings, ideas, reflections:

"Go confidently in the direction of your dreams!
Live the life you've imagined."

-Henry David Thoreau

I am grateful for:

I am:

Focus for the day:

What steps are required to execute my vision?

Thoughts, feelings, ideas, reflections:

"Today I will do what others won't
so tomorrow I can accomplish what others can't."

- Jerry Rice

I am grateful for:

I am:

Focus for the day:

What resources, including information, do I need to achieve my dream?

Thoughts, feelings, ideas, reflections:

"Look closely at the present you are constructing:
it should look like the future you are dreaming."
-Alice Walker

I am grateful for:

I am:

Focus for the day:

How can I obtain those resources?

Thoughts, feelings, ideas, reflections:

"Genius begins great works; labor alone finishes them."

-Joseph Joubert

I am grateful for:

I am:

Focus for the day:

One thing I can accomplish today toward my goal:

Thoughts, feelings, ideas, reflections:

"If you want to win, do the ordinary things better than anyone else does them day in and day out."

-Chuck Noll

I am grateful for:

I am:

Focus for the day:

_____ *is stopping me from achieving my goal, and I am going to overcome that by:*

Thoughts, feelings, ideas, reflections:

"Wherever you are, be there totally. If you find your here and now intolerable and it makes you unhappy, you have three options: remove yourself from the situation, change it, or accept it totally. If you want to take responsibility for your life, you must choose one of those three options, and you must choose now. Then accept the consequences."

-Eckhart Tolle

I am grateful for:

I am:

Focus for the day:

What I can do this week, month, and year to achieve
my goals includes:

Thoughts, feelings, ideas, reflections:

"Do not let what you cannot do interfere with what you can do."
— John Wooden

MY GAME PLAN

(use prose, make a list, create a calendar, or write a checklist)

Week 4

YOUR TEAM

"The supreme quality for leadership is unquestionable integrity. Without it, no real success is possible, no matter whether it is in a section gang, a football field, in an army, or in an office."

Dwight D. Eisenhower

We all need a team to help us execute our game plans. This week, review the members of your team and decide who, if anyone, needs to be cut from the roster. Not everyone is meant to be in your life forever, so your team will inevitably change over time.

This week you will construct your roster with the following positions (and you can always add more):

1 *"road dogs"*: those few people in your life around whom you can let go and completely be yourself and who will hold you accountable and encourage you.

2 *"mentors"*: coaches and individuals who can provide guidance or counsel whether in one situation or for an extended time.

3 *"sponsors"*: people who believe in you and your dream and will take action to support it.

4 *"allies"* or *"strategic partners"*: individuals you can partner with to achieve an element of your dream.

Now, it's time to construct your championship roster.

I am grateful for:

I am:

Focus for the day:

I feel safe around:

Thoughts, feelings, ideas, reflections:

"We are called at certain moments to comfort people who are enduring some trauma. Many of us don't know how to react in such situations, but others do. In the first place, they just show up. They provide a ministry of presence. Next, they don't compare. The sensitive person understands that each person's ordeal is unique and should not be compared to anyone else's. Next, they do the practical things--making lunch, dusting the room, washing the towels. Finally, they don't try to minimize what is going on."

-David Brooks

I am grateful for:

I am:

Focus for the day:

My road dogs who I can recruit to hold me accountable to my plan are:

Thoughts, feelings, ideas, reflections:

"Keep away from those who try to belittle your ambitions. Small people always do that, but the really great make you believe that you too can become great."
-Mark Twain

I am grateful for:

I am:

Focus for the day:

My strategic partners and allies are:

Thoughts, feelings, ideas, reflections:

"Don't always look above you to collaborate.
Look beside you."
-Michael B. Jordan

I am grateful for:

I am:

Focus for the day:

What is the best advice I have received? Who asks me good questions? Who would I like to have as a mentor?

Thoughts, feelings, ideas, reflections:

"Strength and honor are her clothing; and she shall rejoice in time to come. She openeth her mouth with wisdom; and in her tongue is the law of kindness."

-Proverbs 31:25 (KJV)

I am grateful for:

I am:

Focus for the day:

When did someone show me who they were? What did I do with that information?

Thoughts, feelings, ideas, reflections:

"Believe people when they show you who they are. The first time."
-Maya Angelou

I am grateful for:

I am:

Focus for the day:

Who does not support my dreams? Who says unkind things to or about me? Let them go.

Thoughts, feelings, ideas, reflections:

"Love is never any better than the lover. Wicked people love wickedly, violent people love violently, weak people love weakly."

-Toni Morrison

I am grateful for:

I am:

Focus for the day:

I am letting go of what _____
thinks.

I am embracing _____
as a sponsor who supports my dream.

Thoughts, feelings, ideas, reflections:

"What's the greater risk? Letting go of what people think—or letting go
of how I feel, what I believe, and who I am?"

-Brené Brown

MY TEAM
(list your roster, paste pictures of your depth chart)

Road Dogs:

Mentors:

Sponsors:

Strategic Partners:

Week 5

READING THE CLIPS

"Baby, those people can't hold a candle to the light God already has shining on your face. Don't you know who you are?
You are God's child."
-Maya Angelou

This week, you will explore how you process the information coming at you.

There are four types of incoming information:

1 *"warm fuzzies"*: positive information you can use as encouragement without relying upon it for validation (which comes from within).

2 *"constructive criticism/teachable moments"*: negative information you can learn from.

3 *"Bulletin Board material"*: negative information with no learning value from your opponents that you stick on the bulletin board to motivate you without distracting you from your purpose or changing your self-worth.

4 *"noise"*: negative information you should tune out altogether because it does not serve the purpose of making you better. (Beware the noise you create in your own head because you may be telling yourself *stories* conflated with *facts*.)

I am grateful for:

I am:

Focus for the day:

What is a "warm fuzzy" that someone gave me? (Start saving those to refer to on a rainy day.)

Thoughts, feelings, ideas, reflections:

"In everyone's life, at some time, our inner fire goes out. It is then burst into flame by an encounter with another human being. We should all be thankful for those people who rekindle the inner spirit."
- Albert Schweitzer

I am grateful for:

I am:

Focus for the day:

The best constructive criticism I received:

Thoughts, feelings, ideas, reflections:

"Not everything that is faced can be changed,
but nothing can be changed until it is faced."
- James Baldwin

I am grateful for:

I am:

Focus for the day:

What is my Bulletin Board material?

Thoughts, feelings, ideas, reflections:

"When God is ready to promote you, he doesn't take a vote. He doesn't check to see who likes you, who is for you, how popular you are. It's not a vote. It's an appointment."

-Joel Osteen

I am grateful for:

I am:

Focus for the day:

What noise do I need to tune out?

Thoughts, feelings, ideas, reflections:

"I am witnessing myself. I am my own audience."
-Erykah Badu

I am grateful for:

I am:

Focus for the day:

Write a thank-you note to your haters:

Thoughts, feelings, ideas, reflections:

"Most people who are hating on you, they are not worried about where you are. They're worried about where you're going."

-Rep. Elijah Cummings

I am grateful for:

I am:

Focus for the day:

What am I throwing away?

Thoughts, feelings, ideas, reflections:

"Is your cucumber bitter? Throw it away. Are there briars in your path? Turn aside. That is enough. Do not go on and say, 'Why were things of this sort ever brought into the world?'"

-Marcus Aurelius

I am grateful for:

I am:

Focus for the day:

What "warm fuzzy" compliment, feedback, or word of encouragement can I give to someone else today?

Thoughts, feelings, ideas, reflections:

"Words have energy and power with the ability to help, to heal, to hinder, to hurt, to harm, to humiliate, and to humble."

-Yehuda Berg

MY BULLETIN BOARD

Warm Fuzzies

Constructive Criticism

Bulletin Board Material

Noise

Week 6

IN-GAME
ADJUSTMENTS

"Perhaps the earth can teach us, as when everything seems dead and later proves to be alive."
-Pablo Neruda

In sports, you adjust the game plan depending on what the opponent is doing and how the game is going. You have to do the same thing in life. While it is important to plan, life will never go according the plan. The most successful people shake off a bad play in life, learn from it, and make the next play.

This week is all about the comeback.

I am grateful for:

I am:

Focus for the day:

When was I defeated? What was the seed?

Thoughts, feelings, ideas, reflections:

"There is no better [teacher] than adversity. Every defeat, every heartbreak, every loss contains its own seed, its own lesson on how to improve your performance next time."

-Malcolm X

I am grateful for:

I am:

Focus for the day:

When did I give up before I really got to fight? How did it feel? When did I battle for what I believed in? How did it feel?

Thoughts, feelings, ideas, reflections:

"He sets up calamities in the gymnasium to set up your inner ear to hear Him in the crisis. The crisis is just a test. It's not a problem. It's not an issue. It's a gym. It's a training center. It's a workout room. You think the problem is a problem. God just gave you the problem so you would learn to trust Him in dark places."

-Bishop T.D. Jakes

I am grateful for:

I am:

Focus for the day:

When did I select another opportunity? How did I
know I was not quitting?

Thoughts, feelings, ideas, reflections:

"We must be willing to let go of the life we have planned,
so as to accept the life that is waiting for us."
- Joseph Campbell

I am grateful for:

I am:

Focus for the day:

I made the hard, right decision when:

It felt:

I made the easy, wrong decision when:

It felt:

Thoughts, feelings, ideas, reflections:

"Every time you make the hard, right decision, you become a bit more courageous. Every time you make the easy, wrong decision, you become a bit more cowardly."

-Ben Horowitz

I am grateful for:

I am:

Focus for the day:

What is my enthusiasm level?

Thoughts, feelings, ideas, reflections:

"Success is going from failure to failure with no loss of enthusiasm."
-Winston Churchill

I am grateful for:

I am:

Focus for the day:

What is not going according to plan? What do I need to adjust?

Thoughts, feelings, ideas, reflections:

"Success is no accident. It is hard work, perseverance, learning, studying, sacrifice, and most of all, love of what you are doing."

-Pele

I am grateful for:

I am:

Focus for the day:

I can behave like a champion by:

Thoughts, feelings, ideas, reflections:

"Winners act like winners before they're winners. The culture precedes positive results. It doesn't get tacked on as an afterthought on the way to the victory stand. Champions behave like champions before they're champions; they have a winning standard of performance before they're winners."
-Bill Walsh

GAME PLAN ADJUSTMENTS
(chart your progress or write your revised plan)

Week 7

RECOVERY

"Self-care is never a selfish act—it is simply good stewardship of the only gift I have, the gift I was put on earth to offer others."
-Parker Palmer

Recovery is part of any performance training. Just as your body cannot build muscle if you over train without rest, you cannot develop your mental toughness or your success in any part of your life without a recovery regimen.

As you train for greatness in your personal and professional life, an essential part of the process is giving yourself the space to recover from the intensity of everything you face. Resting is not quitting. Self-care is required for battle. Required self-care is physical, mental, and spiritual. Recovery includes sleep, nutrition, hydration, time away from your devices to just think, and—perhaps most importantly—experiences that bring you joy.

I am grateful for:

I am:

Focus for the day:

When I was not taking good care of myself, what were my excuses? How did it feel? How did I change it?

When did I feel amazing?

Thoughts, feelings, ideas, reflections:

"Take care of your body. It is the only place you have to live."
— Jim Rohn

I am grateful for:

I am:

Focus for the day:

Sit quietly with your eyes closed and take 20 deep breaths.

Thoughts, feelings, ideas, reflections:

"Be here now. Be somewhere else later. Is that so complicated?"

-David Bader

I am grateful for:

I am:

Focus for the day:

Even if I don't feel forgiving right now, who do I need to forgive?

Thoughts, feelings, ideas, reflections:

"Resentment is like drinking poison and
waiting for the other person to die."
-Carrie Fisher

I am grateful for:

I am:

Focus for the day:

List at least one technology break to which I will commit and how I will hold myself accountable to the commitment:

Thoughts, feelings, ideas, reflections:

"Knowing how to be solitary is central to the art of loving.
When we can be alone, we can be with others without using them as a means of escape."
-bell hooks

I am grateful for:

I am:

Focus for the day:

What is one way I could rest so I don't quit?

Thoughts, feelings, ideas, reflections:

"If you get tired, learn to rest, not to quit."
-Banksy

I am grateful for:

I am:

Focus for the day:

I am proud I survived:

Something that brings me joy that I can do to celebrate:

Thoughts, feelings, ideas, reflections:

"Never be ashamed of a scar.
It just means you were stronger than whatever tried to hurt you."
-Unknown via Steve Smith, Sr.

I am grateful for:

I am:

Focus for the day:

If I was coming out to the cheer of the crowd, what would be my walkout song?

(Listen to that song today and whenever you are headed to the away game of life, where a hostile crowd is waiting for you.)

Thoughts, feelings, ideas, reflections:

"If you woke up today, you winning."
-2 Chainz

MY RECOVERY REGIMEN

Week 8

PRACTICE

"Our deepest fear is not that we are inadequate. Our deepest fear is that we are powerful beyond measure. It is our light, not our darkness that most frightens us. We ask ourselves, 'Who am I to be brilliant, gorgeous, talented, fabulous?' Actually, who are you not to be? You are a child of God. Your playing small does not serve the world. There is nothing enlightened about shrinking so that other people won't feel insecure around you. We are all meant to shine, as children do. We were born to make manifest the glory of God that is within us. It's not just in some of us; it's in everyone. And as we let our own light shine, we unconsciously give other people permission to do the same. As we are liberated from our own fear, our presence automatically liberates others."

-Marianne Williamson

Congratulations! You made it to the final week: practice. It takes consistent practice to become proficient at anything in life. Over the past seven weeks, you have been practicing being a champion. This final week is designed to cement the daily rituals into your routine so they will carry you beyond the next seven days.

I am grateful for:

I am:

Focus for the day:

Thoughts, feelings, ideas, reflections:

"Get in the habit of asking yourself,
does this support the life I am trying to create?"
-Irisa Yardenah

I am grateful for:

I am:

Focus for the day:

Thoughts, feelings, ideas, reflections:

"You're either feeding your history or feeding your destiny,
but you can't feed both."

- Joel Osteen

I am grateful for:

I am:

Focus for the day:

Thoughts, feelings, ideas, reflections:

"Do you have the patience to wait until your mind settles and the water is clear? Can you remain unmoving until the right action arises by itself?"

-Lao Tzu

I am grateful for:

I am:

Focus for the day:

Thoughts, feelings, ideas, reflections:

"We must always change, renew, rejuvenate ourselves;
otherwise, we harden."

- Johann Wolfgang van Goethe

I am grateful for:

I am:

Focus for the day:

Thoughts, feelings, ideas, reflections:

"There is a fountain of youth; it is your mind, your talents, the creativity you bring to your life and the lives of people you love. When you learn to tap this source, you will have truly defeated age."

-Sophia Loren

I am grateful for:

I am:

Focus for the day:

Thoughts, feelings, ideas, reflections:

"True happiness comes from the joy of deeds well done,
the zest of creating things new."

-Antoine de Saint-Exupery

I am grateful for:

I am:

Focus for the day:

Thoughts, feelings, ideas, reflections:

"Spirit is always there. God's language is silence.
Everything else is poor translation."

-Deepak Chopra

PRACTICE NOTES AND REFLECTIONS
ON THE SZN

Thank you for the honor of coaching you and playing alongside you this #sznofchange

ABOUT THE AUTHOR

Hannah Gordon is an executive, speaker, writer, teacher, and Presidential Leadership Scholar. She serves as the Chief Administrative Officer and General Counsel of the National Football League's San Francisco 49ers. Named one of football's most influential women by NFL.com, Gordon's career started as the first female beat writer for UCLA's *Daily Bruin*. Gordon went on to work for the National Football League's Oakland Raiders, the National Football League Players Association, the University of California at Berkeley, and the National Football League's office in New York, where she was the only woman in a non-secretary role in the salary cap department. She was later dubbed the "Queen of the Lockout" for her role in the 2011 collective bargaining negotiations. Gordon has been named a Sports Business Journal Game Changer, a Legal 500 U.S. Rising Star, a Silicon Valley Business Journal Woman of Influence, and a Corporate Counsel Diversity Champion. Gordon speaks around the country and has been a guest lecturer at Columbia University, University of Pennsylvania's Wharton School of Business, University of California, Berkeley, among others, and has been featured on NFL Network, *SB Nation*, and the *Huffington Post*, among other publications. Gordon holds a B.A. from UCLA and a J.D. from Stanford, where she served as a lecturer in law.